EP Modern History Printables: Levels 5-8

Includes Art and Music

This book belongs to:

_____

This book was made for your convenience. It is available for printing from the Easy Peasy All-in-One Homeschool website. It contains all of the printables from Easy Peasy's modern history course. The instructions for each page are found in the online course.

Easy Peasy All-in-One Homeschool is a free online homeschool curriculum providing high quality education for children around the globe. It provides complete courses for preschool through high school graduation. For EP's curriculum visit allinonehomeschool.com.

EP Modern History Printables: Levels 5-8

ISBN: 9798470813176
First Edition: August 2019

History Timeline Pieces

The First Transcontinental
Railroad
November 6, 1869

George Washington Carver

Thomas Alva Edison
1879

Alexander Graham Bell
1876

Wilbur and Orville Wright
December 17, 1903

Henry Ford
1908

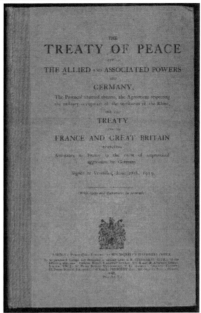

The Treaty of Versailles
June 28, 1919

Assassination of Archduke
Franz Ferdinand
June 28, 1914

Herbert Hoover
31st President
1929-1933

Franklin D. Roosevelt
32nd President
1933-1945

Brown v Board of Education
Topeka, Kansas
1954

March on Washington
August 28, 1963

Harry S Truman

Communism

Apollo 11
July 20, 1969

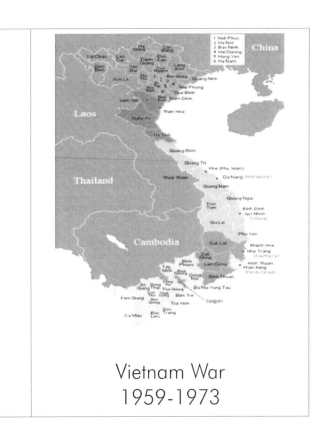

Vietnam War
1959-1973

Berlin Wall
1961-1989

Richard Nixon
1969-1974

Gerald Ford
1974-1977

Jimmy Carter
1977-1981

Ronald Reagan
1981-1989

George H. W. Bush
1989-1993

Bill Clinton
1993-2001

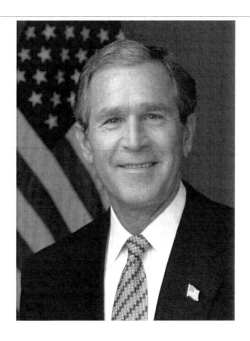

George W. Bush
2001-2009

Barack Obama
2009-2017

War on Terror
2001

Modern History
Timeline pieces

Music Timeline Pieces

Hans Pfitzner

Piotr Tchaikovsky

Sergei Rachmaninoff

Maurice Ravel

Duke Ellington

WWII

Igor Stravinsky

Aaron Copland

Art Timeline Pieces

Henri Matisse

Hector Guimard

Jacob Lawrence
Self Portrait

Pablo Picasso

Jackson Pollock

Max Ernst

Andy Warhol

History

Worksheet Pages

Post-Civil War

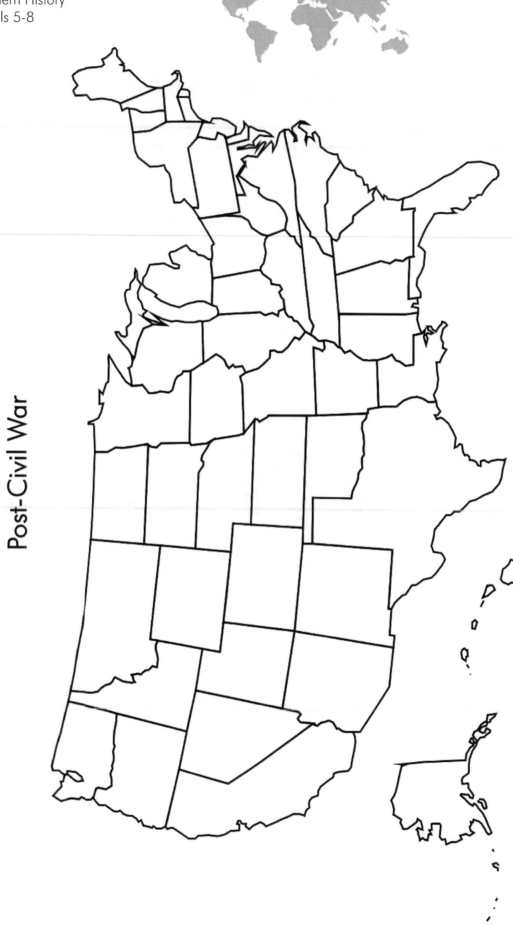

Color a map of the USA to show which states belonged to the United States at the end of the Civil War.

Transcontinental Railroad

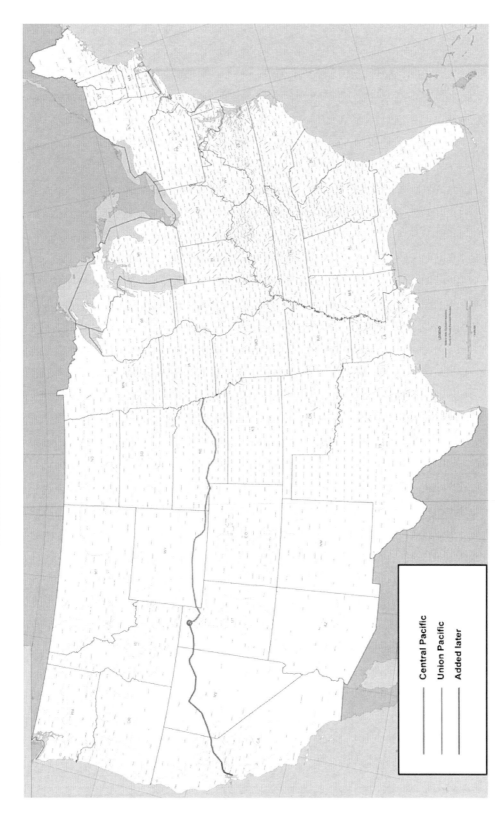

Label each route with the name of the man in charge of that section of railroad.

Central Pacific

Union Pacific

Added later

Coal Miner

Write from the perspective of a coal miner.

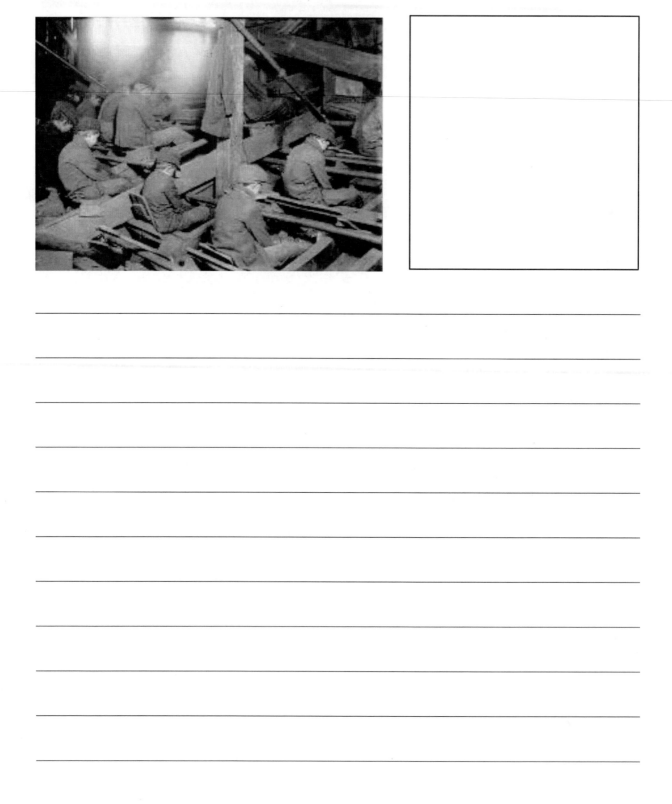

_____

_____

_____

_____

_____

_____

_____

_____

Statue of Liberty

Copy the quote. You can color the picture if you'd like.

"Give me your tired, your poor,
Your huddled masses yearning to breathe free,
The wretched refuse of your teeming shore.
Send these, the homeless, tempest-tossed to me,
I lift my lamp beside the golden door!"

_____

_____

_____

_____

_____

_____

_____

Book Report

Title: _____

Author: _____

Publisher: _____ Date Published: _____

Plot: _____

Setting: _____

Main Character's Name: _____ Age: _____

What is this character like in the beginning?

_____

_____

How has this character changed by the end?

_____

_____

Tell something you learned from this book:

_____

_____

Tell what you liked about the book.

_____

_____

Tell what you didn't like about the book.

_____

_____

Wright Brothers

Draw or write about what you learned.

Amelia Earhart

Write about Amelia Earhart.

_____

_____

_____

_____

_____

_____

_____

Bessie Coleman

Write about Bessie Coleman.

_____

_____

_____

_____

_____

_____

_____

_____

Charles Lindbergh

Write about Charles Lindbergh.

_____

_____

_____

_____

_____

_____

_____

Map

Color in the map and be sure to mark the key!

COLOR KEY	
☐ Turkey	☐ Germany
☐ France	☐ Russia
☐ Serbia	☐ Hungary
☐ Austria	

Map Source: http://d-maps.com/carte.php?num_car=2232&lang=en

Europe

Follow the online directions to complete this map activity.

(Title)

Map source: http://d-maps.com/carte.php?lib=europe_1914_map&num_car=6029&lang=en

World War I

The Crime of the Ages—Who Did It?

Source: John McCutcheon, The Chicago Tribune; H. H. Windsor, Cartoons Magazine (adapted)

Look carefully at the picture. This is a political cartoon about World War I.

Besides all of the soldiers in the middle, who are the other two characters?

_____

The title of the cartoon is, "The Crime of the Ages—Who Did It?"

What crime was committed?

_____

The final character we don't see except the accusing finger.

Each soldier in the middle represents a country. Who is getting most of the blame?

_____

The countries all blame someone else but each has his hand on what?

_____

What is the only country that doesn't seem to have an opinion or any blame?

_____

What do you think is the point of this cartoon?

_____

_____

Current Events

NEWS

Dec 29, 2004 - The Inkscape developers have set a goal for the release of Inkscape 0.41 for mid-late January. There are some noteworthy new features that would be worth getting out to users, and with some major internal changes that will be taking place soon, a good stable release is needed prior to starting such an undertaking.

Dec 29, 2004 - The Inkscape developers have set a goal for the release of Inkscape 0.41 for mid-late January. There are some noteworthy new features that would be worth getting out to users, and with some major internal changes that will be taking place soon, a good stable release is needed prior to starting such an undertaking.

WHAT happened?

_____

_____

_____

_____

_____

_____

WHO was there?

_____

_____

_____

_____

WHY did it happen?

_____

_____

_____

_____

_____

WHEN did it happen?

_____

_____

_____

_____

WHERE did it happen?

_____

_____

_____

_____

_____

Modern History
Levels 5-8

Map Activity

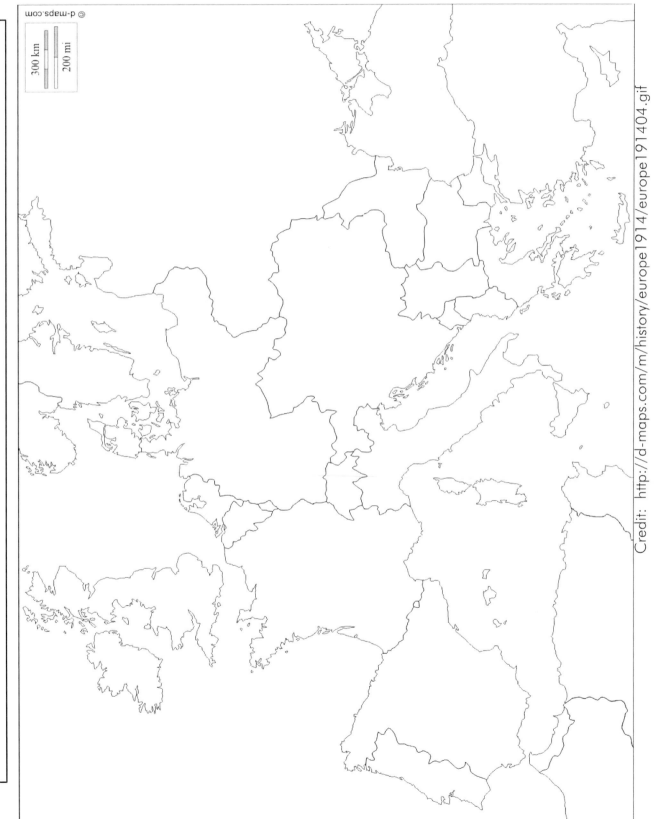

Causes of War

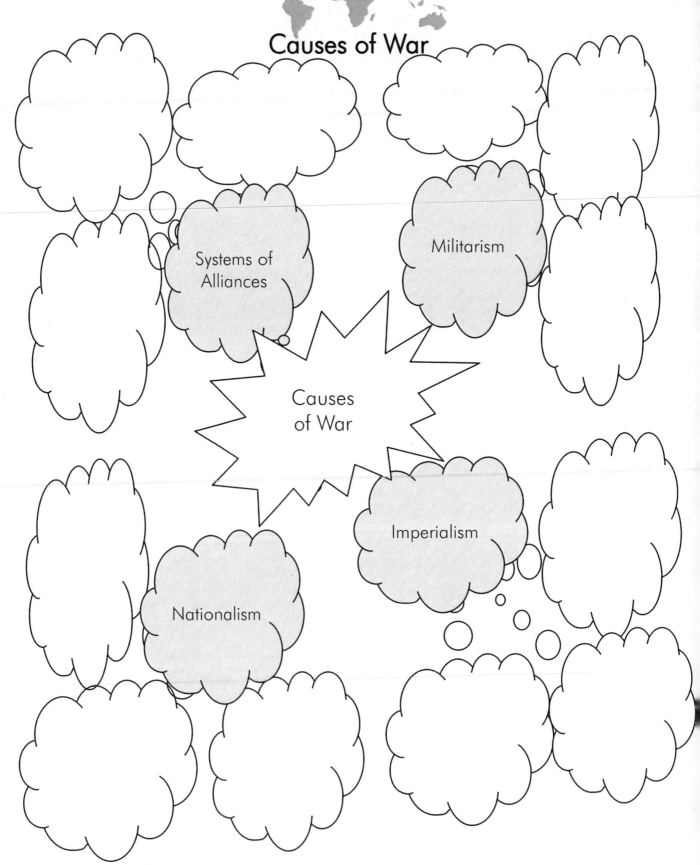

Systems of Alliances

Militarism

Causes of War

Imperialism

Nationalism

World War I

Match the terms and definitions.

_____ 1.	war front	A. the border between Germany/Austria-Hungary and France/Italy
_____ 2.	trench	B. the area that fighting takes place in a war
_____ 3.	naval battle	C. the border between Germany/Austria-Hungary and Russia/Hungary
_____ 4.	"No Man's Land"	D. battles that take place at sea
_____ 5.	Eastern Front	E. the area between the trenches, not belonging to either side
_____ 6.	Western Front	F. long, narrow ditches dug along the front lines, soldiers fought while hidden in the ditches.

Match the World War 1 vehicle name to the description.

_____ 1.	airship	G. German submarine
_____ 2.	triplane	H. large, gas-filled aircraft (without wings) propelled by engines
_____ 3.	tank	I. aircraft with three sets of wings, one over another
_____ 4.	u-boat	J. large, armored vehicle

Match the terms and definitions.

_____ 1.	Allied Powers	K. a focus on building strong armed forces
_____ 2.	Central Powers	L. France, Great Britain, Russia, Italy, Japan
_____ 3.	alliance	M. to not take sides in a war; to not take action to aid either side
_____ 4.	Archduke Ferdinand	N. Germany, Austria-Hungary, Turkey
_____ 5.	assassination	O. agreement between two countries to help/assist each other
_____ 6.	armistice	P. was next in line to be king of Austria when he was assassinated
_____ 7.	surrender	Q. the murder of a leader or important person
_____ 8.	neutral	R. agreement to stop fighting to discuss possible peace
_____ 9.	militarism	S. when one group in a war stops fighting and admits defeat

World War I

Unscramble the letters to make the words that fit the clue. (The numbered letters will reveal a fun fact!)

This term means the building up of strong military forces and gathering weapons
MILTAIMIRS

						4			

This term means the agreement made between two or more countries to defend and aid each other in conflicts with other countries.
CASNELILA

						1		

This term refers to a country's goal of expanding and building an empire. At the time of World War 1, European countries were racing to gain more land in Africa and Asia.
MALMIIPERSI

									6

This term refers to a devotion and pride in one's country. In the extreme, a feeling of superiority over all other countries.
SOIMALTINAN

	5						7		

The Triple Alliance, formed in 1882, joined Germany, _____, and Italy.
SAATURI-HUYGNRA

							-	2					

The Triple _____, formed in 1907, joined Britain, France, and Russia in alliance.
ETNEETN

3						

During World War 1, a carrier pigeon was awarded the Croix de guerre, a military decoration for honor or valor in battle. Even after being shot, he continued to fly to deliver a message that saved 194 soldiers. Fill in the blanks with the letters indicated above to see his name.

1	2	3	4		5	6	7

Graphic Organizer

What happened?

When did it happen?

Where did this take place?

Who was involved?

Why did it happen?

Europe After 1919 (Treaty of Versailles)

Color the map to show what used to be Germany and what used to be Austria-Hungary.

Map source:
Florida Center for Instructional Technology
https://fcit.usf.edu/holocaust/MAPS/map003b.pdf

Venn Diagram

1920s

NOW

The Great Depression

Answer the questions about the Great Depression.

1. Who was the President at the start of the Great Depression?

_____

2. Unemployment rates did NOT account for married _____ who
lost their jobs.

3. What was the name given to the communities of homeless established
during the Great Depression?

_____

4. What event marks the beginning of the Great Depression?

_____

5. Who was elected President during the Great Depression?

_____

6. What was the name given to the reforms and programs implemented by
Roosevelt and Congress?

_____

7. The New Deal created many new government agencies. Name a few and
describe what they did.

_____

_____

_____

_____

_____

_____

Use this space to write a headline announcing President Roosevelt's New Deal
plan.

News Article

Write a 3-5 sentence news article about life during the Great Depression. You could write an article about visiting the Hoovervilles or a soup kitchen.

Did you write a complete article?
Who is the article about? What happened? When did it take place?
Where did it happen? Why is it important?

Animal Farm

Write a description of how the animals' leaders were able to carry out the revolution.

Animal Farm symbol

Soviet symbol

Axis and Allies

World with Countries - Outline by FreeVectorMaps.com

Key:

World Leaders

World War II

LEAVE THIS TO US
SONNY — **YOU OUGHT**
TO BE OUT OF LONDON

MINISTRY OF HEALTH EVACUATION SCHEME

What do you think
of the evacuation
of children during
World War II?

_____

_____

_____

_____

_____

Treaty of Versailles

Look at this political cartoon and answer the questions below.

What is the cartoon about?

_____

What is each person and object in the image and what do they represent?

_____

What is the load and what has it caused the horse to do? What does that represent?

_____

_____

What is the author's message?

_____

_____

Map Activity

Follow the online directions to complete the map activity.

_____

(Title)

Map Source:

https://d-maps.com/carte.php?num_car=4572&lang=en

Political Cartoon

Look at this political cartoon and answer the questions below.

What do the two birds represent? _____

_____

What is each doing? _____

_____

_____

What is the meaning of what the American bird is saying? _____

_____

What is the author's message? _____

_____

The Blitz

Fill in this news organizer for an article on the Blitz.

Dec 29, 2004 - The Inkscape developers have set a goal for the release of Inkscape 0.41 for mid-late January. There are some noteworthy new features that would be worth getting out to users, and with some major internal changes that will be taking place soon, a good stable release is needed prior to starting such an undertaking.

Dec 29, 2004 - The Inkscape developers have set a goal for the release of Inkscape 0.41 for mid-late January. There are some noteworthy new features that would be worth getting out to users, and with some major internal changes that will be taking place soon, a good stable release is needed prior to starting such an undertaking.

WHAT happened?

_____

_____

_____

WHO was there?

_____

_____

_____

WHY did it happen?

_____

_____

_____

WHEN did it happen?

_____

_____

WHERE did it happen?

_____

_____

_____

World War II

World War II significantly affected the economy. Prices for common goods had increased greatly during the war. The government also started selling war savings bonds to help fund the war efforts.

This poster was popular in Britain during World War II. Read this poster and answer the questions below.

Who is represented in the cartoon? _____

_____

What is the message?

_____

_____

What action did the author want women to take?

_____

How would that help?

_____

_____

Anne Frank

_____

_____

_____

_____

_____

_____

_____

_____

_____

_____

_____

_____

_____

_____

_____

Who? What? Where? When? Why?

Fill in this organizer with information about the attack on Pearl Harbor.

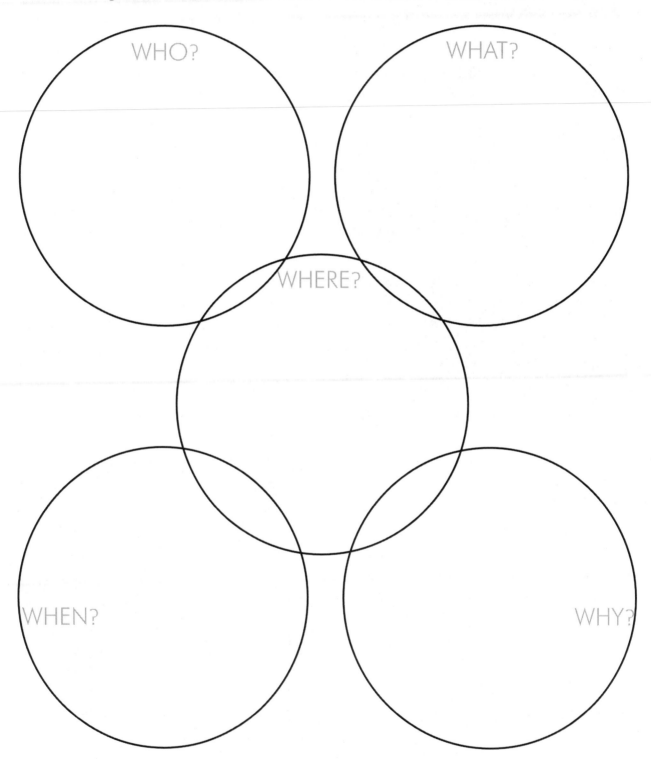

WHO?

WHAT?

WHERE?

WHEN?

WHY?

War in the Pacific

Fill in the blanks using words from the Word Bank.

In 1940, _____ joined the Axis alliance, joining with Germany and Italy.

On December 7th, 1941, Japan attacked _____ _____.

Immediately following this attack, the United States of America joined in the alliance with the _____.

In June 1942, the United States won the _____ ____ _____ by sinking several Japanese aircraft carriers.

A famous statue of Marines raising the American flag commemorates another important battle that took place on the island of _____ _____.

In August of 1945, the United States President Harry Truman made the decision to use the _____ _____, a newly designed weapon. These were dropped on the cities of Hiroshima and Nagasaki in Japan.

This action caused Japan to _____. A treaty was signed on September 2, 1945, now known as V-J Day (which means _____ ____ _____).

Word Bank	
Victory in Japan	Pearl Harbor
Iwo Jima	Japan
Allies	Battle of Midway
surrender	atomic bomb

Attack on Pearl Harbor

Use this space to write about what you have learned about the Pearl Harbor attack.

_____

_____

_____

_____

_____

_____

_____

_____

Color Japan red and color Pearl Harbor (Hawaii) blue.

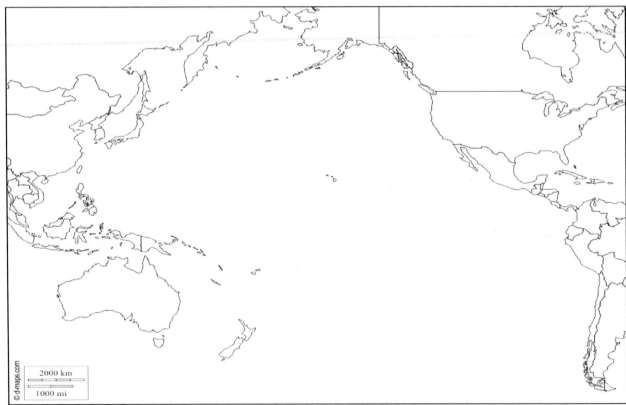

(Map source: https://d-maps.com/carte.php?num_car=3261&lang=en)

Political Cartoon

Answer the questions about the cartoon.

We Always Were Suckers for Ridiculous Hats . . .

Why did Americans seem to "have their heads in the sand?"
How did the attack on Pearl Harbor effectively pull American's head out?

_____

_____

_____

_____

_____

China

World War II

Geneva Convention & Japanese Prison Camps	Battle of Dunkirk

Blitzkreig

U boats	Topic: _____

Topic: _____	Topic: _____

D Day

The men in the water were just on that ship. What are they doing?

_____

This was on D-Day. When was that?

_____

What was D-Day?

_____

What was the outcome?

_____

Describe D-Day.

_____

_____

VE Day

What is happening in this picture?

_____

Why?

_____

When was VE Day?

_____

What marked the end of the war in Europe?

_____

Dr. Martin Luther King, Jr.
Webquest

1929	When and where was Martin Luther King, Jr. born?
1953	Who did Martin Luther King, Jr. marry?
1954	Dr. Martin Luther King, Jr. became pastor of which church?
1955	Martin Luther King, Jr. was spokesman for a specific non-violent protest. What was the name of the non-violent protest?
1963	What famous speech did Martin Luther King, Jr. deliver? Where did this take place?
1964	What honor was he awarded?
1968	Where and how did Dr. Martin Luther King, Jr. die?

From what you have read, describe Martin Luther King, Jr.'s dream. _____

_____

_____

_____

_____

Political Cartoons

<u>Look closely at this cartoon.</u>

Who is represented by the eagle?

_____

Who is represented by the bear?

_____

What is creating the chasm between them?

_____

What does this cartoon show about the

relationship between former allies?

_____

<u>Here is another Dr. Seuss political cartoon. You may remember seeing a cartoon</u>

<u>by him about how America didn't want to get involved in WWII. Look at this Cold</u>

<u>War cartoon.</u>

Who is represented by the man in the first bed?

_____

Who is in the second bed?

_____

What is meant by "the gap?"

_____

What is meant by the caption under the cartoon?

_____

What is it that the man is happy he won't catch?

_____

What is the point of the cartoon?_____

Notebooking Page

1918
Billy Graham born in Charlotte, NC

Billy Graham made his commitment to Jesus

Graham graduated from FL Bible Institute

1943

1945

1957
Graham received a star on the Hollywood Walk of Fame

1996
Billy Graham awarded the

Billy Graham died at the age of 99

End of WWI

1939
Britain declared war on Germany, WWII began

US dropped atomic bombs on Japan, WWII ended

1954
Brown vs Board of Education, ruled against "separate but equal"

Montgomery Bus Boycott began

1961
Russians put the first man in space: Yuri Gagarin

President Kennedy assassinated

Dr. Martin Luther King, Jr. assassinated

Neil Armstrong became first man to walk on the moon

Timeline Clues:

1. World War I ended the same year Billy Graham was born. Sixteen years later, Billy Graham made a personal commitment to Christ.

2. Billy Graham graduated from FL Bible Institute the year after World War II began. Three years later, he married Ruth McCue Bell.

3. World War II ended in 1945. In the same year, Billy Graham became the charter vice president of Youth for Christ International.

4. One year after the Brown vs Board of Education ruling, Dr. Martin Luther King Jr. was involved in a non-violent protest in 1955. Two years later, Billy Graham led a 16-week crusade in New York City.

5. When the Russians succeeded in getting a man into space, President Kennedy was determined the US would get a man on the moon. Neil Armstrong landed on the moon in 1969, six years after President Kennedy was assassinated.

6. Dr. Martin Luther King Jr. was assassinated 5 years after President Kennedy's assassination.

7. Twenty years after Neil Armstrong walked on the moon, Billy Graham received a star on the Hollywood Walk of Fame. Seven years after that, Billy Graham was awarded the Congressional Gold Medal.

8. Billy Graham died at the age of 99 in 2018.

Political Cartoon

Look at this political cartoon and answer the questions below.

Who are the men and what countries do they represent?

_____

What are they sitting on? What do they represent?

_____

What are they doing? What does that represent?

_____

What are the men's other hands poised to do? What does

that represent?

_____

What's the message of the cartoon?

_____

Current Events

Dec 29, 2004 - The Inkscape developers have set a goal for the release of Inkscape 0.41 for mid-late January. There are some noteworthy new features that would be worth getting out to users, and with some major internal changes that will be taking place soon, a good stable release is needed prior to starting such an undertaking.

Dec 29, 2004 - The Inkscape developers have set a goal for the release of Inkscape 0.41 for mid-late January. There are some noteworthy new features that would be worth getting out to users, and with some major internal changes that will be taking place soon, a good stable release is needed prior to starting such an undertaking.

WHAT happened?

_____

_____

_____

_____

_____

WHO was there?

_____

_____

_____

_____

_____

WHY did it happen?

_____

_____

_____

_____

_____

WHEN did it happen?

_____

_____

_____

_____

_____

WHERE did it happen?

_____

_____

_____

_____

_____

Research Report Note Taker

Topic: _____

Resource 1: _____

Info: _____   Info: _____

Info: _____   Info: _____

Info: _____   Info: _____

Resource 2: _____

Info: _____   Info: _____

Info: _____   Info: _____

Info: _____   Info: _____

Resource 3: _____

Info: _____   Info: _____

Info: _____   Info: _____

Info: _____   Info: _____

Resource 4: _____

Info: _____   Info: _____

Info: _____   Info: _____

Info: _____   Info: _____

Resource 5: _____

Info: _____   Info: _____

Info: _____   Info: _____

Info: _____   Info: _____

Resource 6: _____

Info: _____   Info: _____

Info: _____   Info: _____

Info: _____   Info: _____

Resource 7: _____

Info: _____   Info: _____

Info: _____   Info: _____

Info: _____   Info: _____

Resource 8: _____

Info: _____   Info: _____

Info: _____   Info: _____

Info: _____   Info: _____

Resource 9: _____

Info: _____   Info: _____

Info: _____   Info: _____

Info: _____   Info: _____

Music

Worksheet Pages

Instrument Families

Put each instrument into the correct family.

Instruments		
Oboe	Viola	Clarinet
French horn	Saxophone	Tuba
Xylophone	Bass drum	Trumpet
Snare drum	Gong	Bassoon
Double bass	Cello	Flute
Violin	Cymbals	Trombone

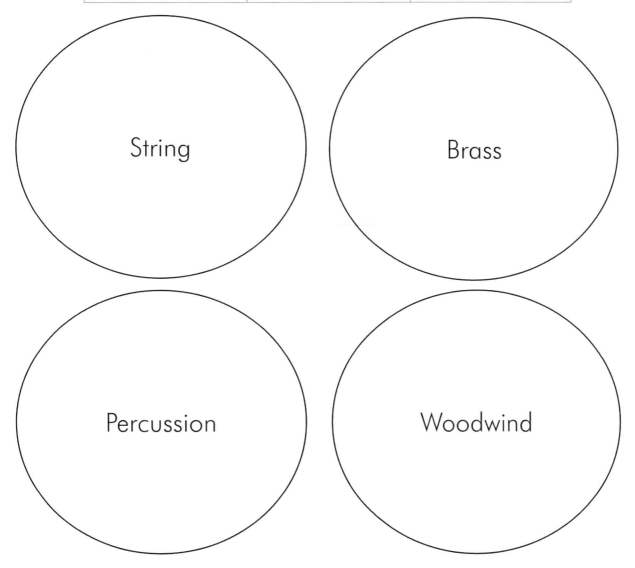

Instrument Families

Choose a color for each instrument family. Then color the area or areas that the instruments in that family would be found.

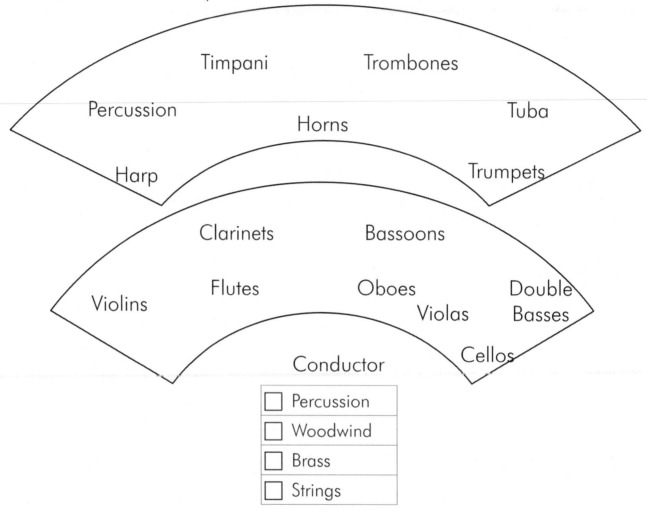

Timpani   Trombones

Percussion   Tuba
                Horns

Harp   Trumpets

Clarinets   Bassoons

        Flutes   Oboes   Double
Violins   Violas   Basses
                                Cellos

Conductor

☐	Percussion
☐	Woodwind
☐	Brass
☐	Strings

What is your favorite instrument and which family does it belong to?

_____

Instrument Identification

Identify these instruments. Give the name of the instrument, the family it belongs to, and describe how it makes music.

_____

_____

_____

_____

_____

_____

_____

_____

_____

_____

_____

_____

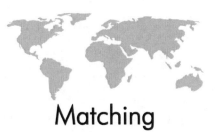

Matching

Match the description to the picture of the instrument.

A member of the string family
Second largest and second lowest pitch of
bowed string instruments

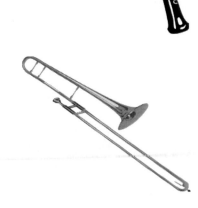

A member of the percussion family
Sounds are from wooden bars struck with mallets

A member of the brass family
Has a sliding section to vary the pitch

A member of the woodwind family
Uses a double reed
Highest octave range of reeded woodwinds

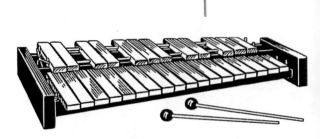

Art

Worksheet Pages

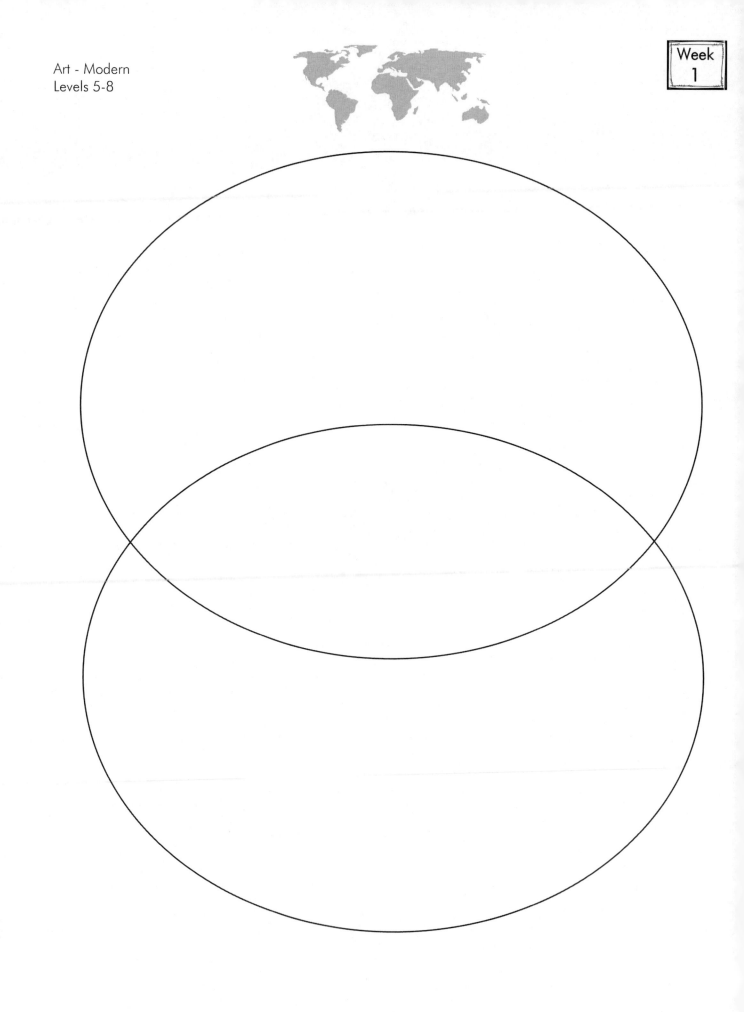

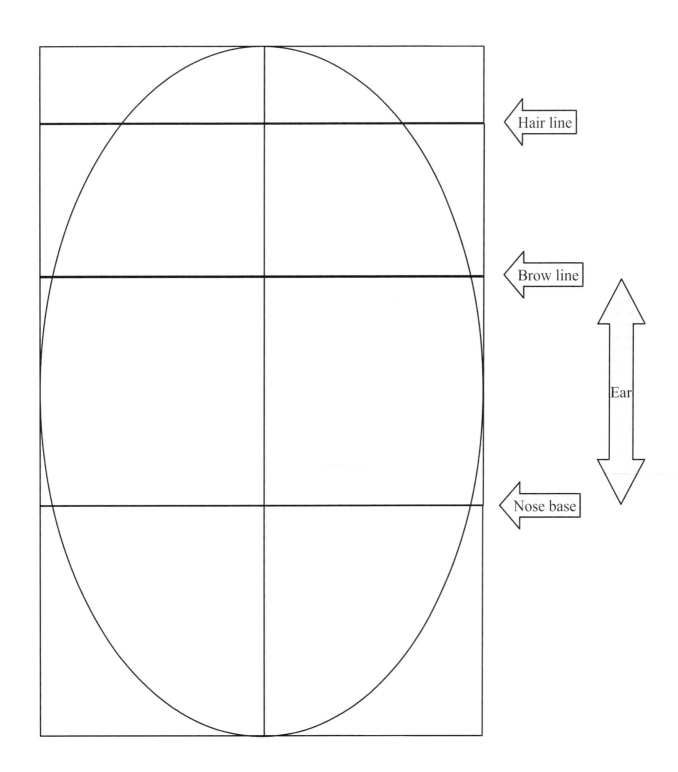

Hair line

Brow line

Ear

Nose base

Bible

Worksheets

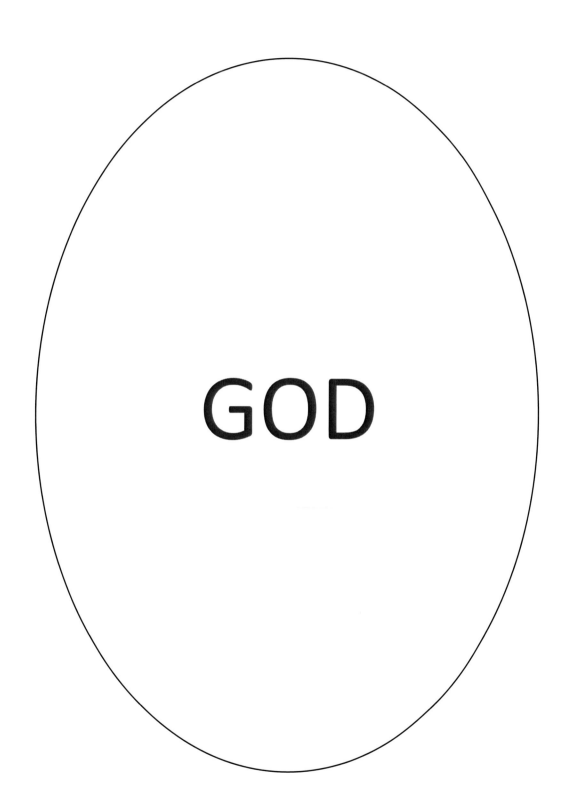

GOD

Made in United States
North Haven, CT
15 July 2024

54828338R00065